FOR FEMALE SINGERS

'80s G[...]

T0040860

CONTENTS

PAGE	TITLE	DEMO TRACK	SING-ALONG TRACK
2	**CALL ME** Blondie	1	2
6	**FLASHDANCE…WHAT A FEELING** Irene Cara	3	4
14	**GIRLS JUST WANT TO HAVE FUN** Cyndi Lauper	5	6
16	**HOW WILL I KNOW** Whitney Houston	7	8
20	**MATERIAL GIRL** Madonna	9	10
24	**MICKEY** Toni Basil	11	12
28	**STRAIGHT UP** Paula Abdul	13	14
9	**WALKING ON SUNSHINE** Katrina and the Waves	15	16

ISBN 0-634-07932-8

HAL•LEONARD®
CORPORATION
7777 W. BLUEMOUND RD. P.O. BOX 13819 MILWAUKEE, WI 53213

Visit Hal Leonard Online at
www.halleonard.com

Call Me

from the Paramount Motion Picture AMERICAN GIGOLO
Words by Deborah Harry
Music by Giorgio Moroder

an - y - time. _ Call me. ___ My love. ___ When you're

ready we can share the wine. _ Call me.

Bridge

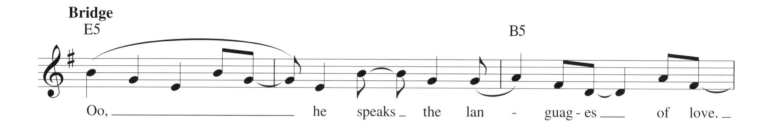

Oo, _____ he speaks _ the lan - guag - es _ of love. _

_ Oo, _____ a - more _ le chia -

- ma - mi. ___ *Spoken:* Chia - ma - mi.

Oo, _____ ap - pelle _ moi mon che - rie. _ *Spoken:* Ap-pelle

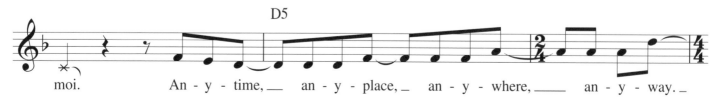

moi. An - y - time, _ an - y - place, _ an - y - where, ___ an - y - way.

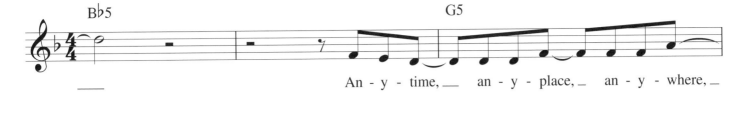

An - y - time, __ an - y - place, __ an - y - where, __

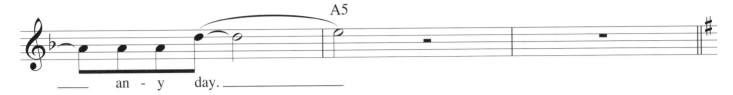

__ an - y day. _____

Synth Solo

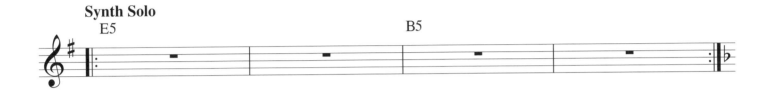

Call me, __

Chorus

__ my love. __ Call me. Call __ me an - y,

an - y - time. __ Call me _____ for a ride. __

Repeat and fade

__ Call me. Call __ me for some o - ver - time. __ Call me, __

Flashdance...What a Feeling

from the Paramount Picture FLASHDANCE
Lyrics by Keith Forsey and Irene Cara
Music by Giorgio Moroder

Additional Lyrics

3. Now, I hear the music,
   Close my eyes, I am rhythm.
   In a flash it takes hold of my heart.

Walking on Sunshine

Words and Music by Kimberley Rew

Intro
Moderately fast

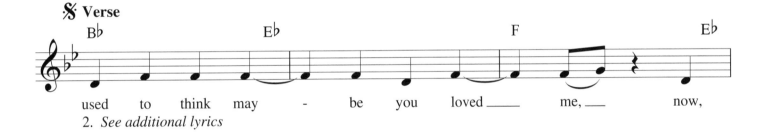

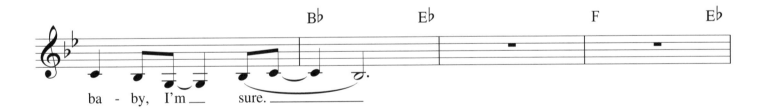

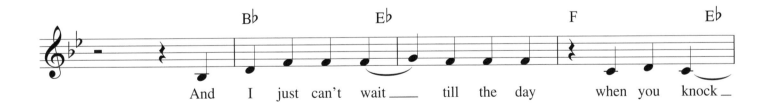

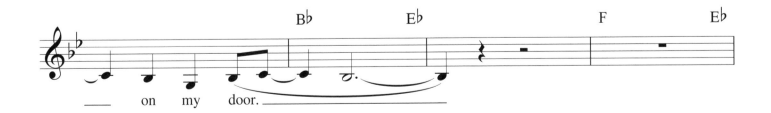

- shine. Whoa, ____ and don't it feel __ good?

Hey. All __ right, now. And don't it feel __ good?

D.S. al Coda 1

Hey. Yeah. ____ 2. I

Coda 1

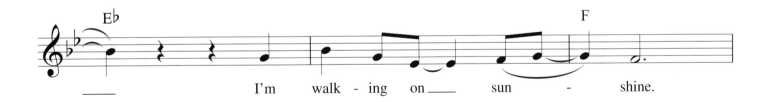

walk - ing on __ sun - shine. Whoa, ____

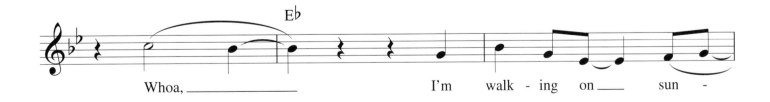

____ I'm walk - ing on __ sun - shine.

Whoa, ____ I'm walk - ing on __ sun -

- shine. Whoa, ____ and

11

To Coda 2 ⊕

Interlude

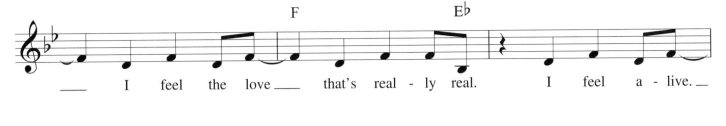

I feel the love ___ that's real - ly real. I feel a - live. ___

I feel the love. ___ I feel the love ___ that's real - ly real.

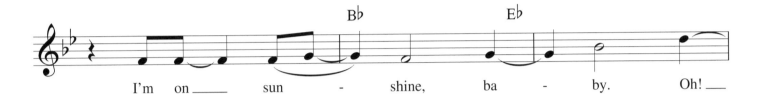

I'm on ___ sun - shine, ba - by. Oh! ___

Oh, yeah. ___ I'm on ___ sun - shine, ba -

D.S.S. al Coda 2

- by. Oh! ___ I'm walk - ing on ___ sun -

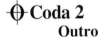 **Coda 2**

Outro

w/ Voc. ad lib., till fade

Repeat and fade

Hey, ___ yeah, _ now. And don't it feel _ good?

Additional Lyrics

2. I used to think maybe you loved me,
   Now I know that it's true.
   And I don't want to spend my whole life
   Just a waiting for you.
   Now I don't want you back for the weekend,
   Not back for a day. Uh, no, no, no.
   I said, baby, I just want you back
   And I want you to stay. Whoa, yeah, now.

Girls Just Want to Have Fun

Words and Music by Robert Hazard

Intro

Bright Rock

*Recording sounds 1/2 step lower than written.

Verse

1. I come home in the morn-ing light. My moth-
2., 3. *See additional lyrics*

- er says, "When you gon-na live your life right?"

Oh, Ma-ma dear, we're not the for-tu-nate ones. And

girls, they want to have fu - un. Oh,

1.
girls just want to have fun. Ah.

2.

Chorus

girls just want to have... That's all they real-ly want

Additional Lyrics

2. The phone rings in the middle of the night.
   My father yells, "What you gonna do with your life?"
   Oh, Daddy dear, you know you're still number one.
   But girls, they want to have fu-un.
   Oh, girls just want to have...

3. Some boys take a beautiful girl
   And hide her away from the rest of the world.
   I want to be the one to walk in the sun.
   Oh, girls, they want to have fu-un.
   Oh, girls just want to have...

How Will I Know

Words and Music by George Merrill, Shannon Rubicam and Narada Michael Walden

Additional Lyrics

2. Oo, I lose control;
   Can't seem to get enough.
   When I wake from dreamin',
   Tell me, is it really love?

3. Oh, wake me; I'm shakin'.
   Wish I had you near me now.
   Said there's no mistakin';
   What I feel is really love.
   Ooh, tell me;...

Material Girl

Words by Peter Brown and Robert Rans

Intro
Moderately

C7sus4   C   C7sus4   C

Play 4 times

Verse

C · · · · · · · · · · · Bb

1. Some boys kiss__ me, some __ boys hug __ me. I _____ think they're O. K. __
3. *See additional lyrics*

Am · · · · · · · C

__ If they don't give __ me prop - er cred - it I __

G7sus4/D   G7sus4   C   **𝄋 Verse**   C

__ just walk __ a - way. _____   2. They can beg __ and they __
                                   4., 5. *See additional lyrics*

Bb · · · · · · · Am

__ can plead __ but they __ can't see the light. _____ (That's right.)

C · · · · · · · G7sus4/D   G7sus4

'Cause the boy __ with the cold __ hard cash __ is al - ways Mis - ter Right. __

Chorus

'Cause we are liv - ing in a ma - te - ri - al world _ and I _

_ am a ma - te - ri - al girl. _ You know _ that we are liv - ing in a ma -

To Coda

te - ri - al world _ and I _ am a ma - te - ri - al girl. _

1.

2.

Bridge

(Liv - ing in a ma -

Ma - te - ri - al.

te - ri - al world. Liv - ing in a ma - te - ri - al world.

a ma-te-ri-al,   a ma-te-ri-al,   a ma-te-ri-al

Outro

world.
(Liv - ing in a ma - te - ri - al world. Liv - ing in a ma- Ma- te - ri - al.

te - ri - al world. Liv - ing in a ma - te - ri - al world. Ma- te - ri -

al, al. te - ri - al world.)
Liv - ing in a ma - te - ri - al world.) te - ri - al world.)

Additional Lyrics

3. Some boys romance, some boys slow dance.
That's all right with me.
If they can't raise my int'rest
Then I have to let them be.

4. Some boys try and some boys lie
But I don't let them play.
Only boys who save their pennies
Make my rainy day.

5. Boys may come and boys may go and
That's all right, you see.
Experience has made me rich
And now they're after me.
'Cause ev'rybody's living...

Mickey

Words and Music by Michael Chapman and Nicky Chinn

D.C. al Coda

Additional Lyrics

2. Now, when you take me by the hand who's ever gonna know?
Ev'ry time you move I let a little more show.
There's somethin' you can use so don't say no, Mickey.
So come on and give it to me any way you can.
Any way you want to do it, I'll take it like a man.
Please, baby, please, don't leave me in this jam, Mickey.

Straight Up

Words and Music by Elliot Wolff

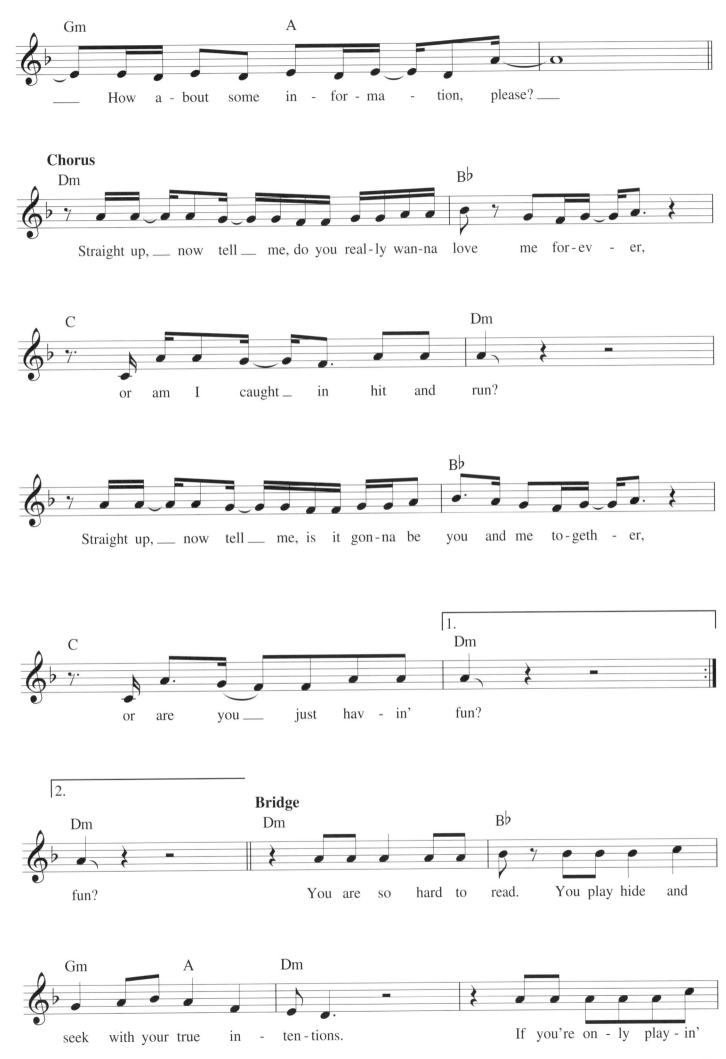

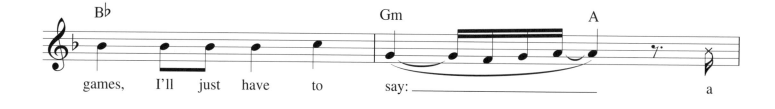

games, I'll just have to say: _____ a

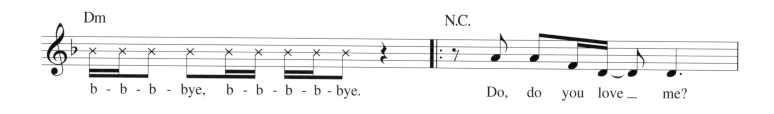

b - b - b - bye, b - b - b - b - bye. Do, do you love ___ me?

Do, do you love ___ me?

Pre-Chorus

A tell me, ba - by. I've been fooled be - fore; ___ would-n't like ___

___ to get my love caught in the slam - min' door. ___ Are you more than hot for me, or

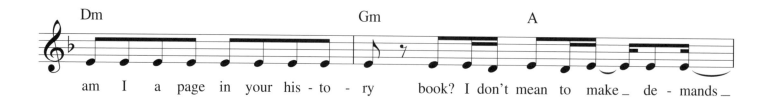

am I a page in your his - to - ry book? I don't mean to make ___ de - mands ___

___ but the word and the deed go hand ___ in hand. ___ How a-bout some in - for - ma - tion,

Additional Lyrics

2. Time's standing still
   Waiting for some small clue.
   A let me tell you how I keep getting chills
   When I think your love is true.

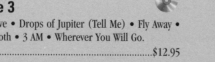